# TO YOU
## *in the*
# NIGHT

# TO YOU
## *in the*
# NIGHT

CARTON

ARCHWAY
PUBLISHING

Archway Publishing books may be ordered through booksellers or by contacting:

Archway Publishing
1663 Liberty Drive
Bloomington, IN 47403
www.archwaypublishing.com
1 (888) 242-5904

ISBN: 978-1-4808-9153-1 (sc)
ISBN: 978-1-4808-9152-4 (hc)
ISBN: 978-1-4808-9154-8 (e)

Library of Congress Control Number: 2020912161

Print information available on the last page.

Archway Publishing rev. date: 07/08/2020

To love or have loved, that is enough.
—Victor Hugo, *Les Misérables*

I was standing
under a mulberry tree
down by the creek
when I first realized
that something was
missing.

The leaves were changing
and I'd just come back,
back from
a distant ocean,
from where mountains and high deserts
and all kinds of old treasures
remain.

But something was aching
within me,
festering,
like a splinter.

I've never felt this way before.

The tea is bitter;
the sky is gray—
what is happening?
I can't even write
anymore.

My bed is warm,
the blankets soft;
a breeze in the window
and the cat on the dresser.

All is good and calm.
The sun plays at the
sill;
the birds at the feeder
come and go
at will.

Why am I crying?

The colors bled away
across the floor
at end of day.
I'm usually just waking,
and my soul starts to dance.
But tonight
is different;
my heels don't fit right
no matter my stance,
and my hair won't curl
either.

So I went to bed
instead.

The doctor had nothing to say,
nothing to prescribe;
I'm healthy as can be.

Read 12:03 AM

CARTON

I kissed him heavy,
hungry,
but something wasn't right,
like
that vinegar smell
when you open the bread,
or when the morning
sky is stained
bright red.

So I pulled back first,
and
we didn't text again.

Another poem
wrung out and done,
and time enough for the setting sun.

I felt (for a moment)
as if my self was back.

So why is everything staying
white and black?

Everything looks the way
bile tastes,
and everything tastes the way
a blizzard feels,
but now
I think I'm onto something.

The neighbor's dog barks
at night,
but it doesn't wake me.
Neither does the highway
one road over
or the garbage man in the morn—

likely because

I don't sleep anymore.

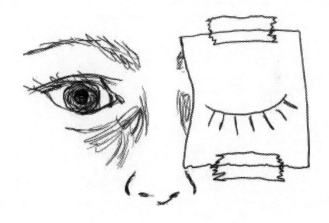

There was a boy:
he kissed me too hard
at a frat party back
in the muddy front yard,
and I hadn't drunk a thing—
but the bruises felt like
*something*
for
once.

It's 2 a.m.
and raining outside ...

I think it's time
for a trip.

The sequoias I pass through
mean less and less.
They only hide what is behind,
no longer a marvel
and more a distraction.
They whisper through my window,
*We saw you long ago;*
*you passed through this air.*

And I keep driving.

A fling here and a fling there,
a half-hearted shot at forever,
but nothing stung until
today.
Nothing hurt until just now,
and I find myself
halfway to Nashville,
wondering if you
are feeling the same way.

You.

I never considered you before.

You were something
at family gatherings,
an idea,
a hassle, an excuse,
something to sigh over
as they all turned their heads,
something that pinched and itched and
dug,
something I always
brushed
under the rug.

I don't know
how, but
I missed the signs.

The truth is,
you have been in
everything;
the possibility of
you
has been a part
of every decision
I have ever
made.

I told them
every time
that it wasn't
for me.

I don't want to be controlled
or bridled
or burdened;
I want to chase the
setting sun
and every maverick
too.
But I realized suddenly
that all these splendid things
might be prettier
to chase
with you.

I'm in a skyscraper
(we don't have them
where I live),
and when I look down
at the hundreds below,
I wonder if I am truly
as alone
as I feel.

Listen:
I don't want you because of
them or
for what they say.
No,
instead
I'd like to hide you
away
and keep
you just for
myself,
not out of shame, mind,
but
to protect something new.

The words won't come.
They've never failed me before.

I've always had something to say,
something to do.
There was always a truth to relay
or a story to brew.

There has always been a distraction,
a place to be,
a journey to take.

But then there was
nothing but
you.

Every time I drag a finger
over the windowpane
through the moisture,
I think of touching you,
of dragging sparks across
your skin.

I think of
you,
you,
*you*
when I am at work
surrounded by stories,
surrounded by legends and myths
and fairy tales
of old.

I know that
one day

we will be
the greatest of them
all.

My book is waiting.

I can hear it whispering,
my characters restlessly murmuring,
*What about us? Where is our happy ending?*

But these days
I am busy wondering about
my own.

I have always walked the line,
always striven
to be the best, the brightest …

What about the books, the pictures,
the food in the fridge?
What about the trail,
the one I walk alone,
high and away
on my own secret ridge?

It's time for a trip.

I pack my things and draw up the plans;
this is not one of my usual ventures.

I have always been a student
on my quests,
stopping and learning along the way,
but this time,
I want nothing more than to
forget everything
I ever knew.

I had a boyfriend once
when I was young and idyllic,
when I sought after nothing
more than I had, and
I was happy;
oh, I was happy,
I was happy …
*Yes?*
I was content
with watching his every move,
waiting for him to visit her
again,
looking for chinks that
I'd created
in our armor.

I haven't tried to love
ever since.

I loved the idea
of love:
I loved the notion
of forever,
of our unnamed children
playing
in his family's
fields,
the security of that
life,
of learning his mother's
cooking
and joining his
father's business.

But I didn't
love *him*,
and that is why
it didn't last.

CARTON

I have learned
that
you may fit
perfectly with someone,
you may slide
right into their
empty spaces,
but
just because the pieces
fit
does not mean that
you are from
the same
puzzle.

He was not the one
I was meant for,
and
I was not the one
he was meant for.

I didn't deserve him, and
he didn't deserve me.

Who you want and
who you are
meant for
start off as two
different people.

After enough heartache,
after enough bleeding
and lessons learned,
they become
the same
person.

We cheated each other.

He went to her room
at the hotel in the city;
I went and fasted
to make myself pretty.
He never gave me flowers,
so I gave him mine,
and now he's happy,
so I made myself
say,

"I'm fine."

The road turned to gravel
in a blink, so quickly
my brakes faltered,
and I remembered what it felt like
to try and stop,
to try and stop missing the last one,
how long it had taken,
how no one had shown up to
save me
from my spiral.

I drive on.

The sky isn't always blue.

It can be angry and red,
it can be pale as the dead,
it can be yellow with storms
as the tornado forms;
the sky can be black
with stars forward and back,
but
for some reason,
I once
named it after you,

and I called the sky blue.

  - to "Blue"

There was a man
at the museum, sweeping.
He paused by me as I stared
up at a painting,
breath halting, perplexed.

"Do you see the anchor?"
he asked.

I squinted, eyes dry enough
at last.
"No, sir. I don't."

"Ah," he laughed
and pushed at his broom.
"Artwork is like that.
No one ever sees
the same thing."

He looked at me, finally.

"Don't you wonder
if maybe
people
are that way
too?
Maybe
each person
sees something different
in you?"

Sorrow is like clay.

If you are patient
enough,
if you take your time,
you can turn such
a
miserable mess
into something
beautiful.

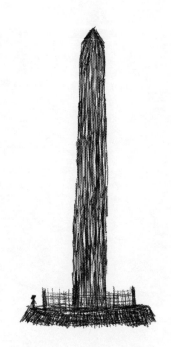

CARTON

Sioux
City
has a
monument,
an obelisk
for a dead
adventurer
who was my
age and some.

I stopped there.

I parked under it and
looked west for a while.

In the shadow
of that monument,
I began to wonder
if I missed my chance
with you,
if maybe you were a hero
in another time
and I am only just getting here
today.

What if they painted you
and lost you?
What if
you are tucked away
in some attic?
What if
only your handwriting
remains?

Only the stars above know
what I want to tell you;
after all,
they've seen this
story a thousand times
before.

I learned a word
today
while studying
pottery:

*Kintsugi.*

Our souls are friends
the way stars
are friends:
we are
far from each other
but part
of the same
constellation.

There are so many
things I want to show you
and
so many things I
am terrified you'll
see.

I am strong,
but Atlas would laugh
and shrug easily,
like the boy at the checkout
downtown.

I am smart, yes,
but nothing Athena would
search out, my mouth
without a sharp edge
and my wit just as dull.

I am decent enough
to look at, though,
all milky skin and fertile curves,
but Aphrodite's temple is dusty,
and no one worships there
anymore.

Who is to say
that I am enough
these days

after all?

Who are you?
Are you across the sea,
staring back,
waiting for me?
Are you at the back of the line?
Did you hold the door for me
last week,
last year?

Maybe, perhaps,
you are content
with
not searching for me yet.

If that's the case, then
I hope we meet

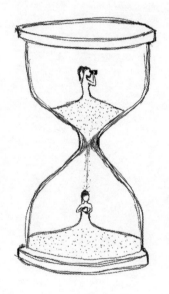

when you're ready
and not a moment sooner.

We will meet in due
time and see
that our time apart
was for the best.
Maybe we will laugh
and agree
that
both of us
had growing to do.

This is important
and true
because
I belong to me
first,
and you belong to
you.

I have been so busy
slaying my dragons,
tearing through myself
like a hurricane,
searching for answers,
that I forgot
it's okay
to be saved
once in a while.

    *—Some demons we cannot conquer alone.*

I hated the idea of
princesses
until
I wanted
someone
to treat
me like one.
I despised glitter and gold
until
I wanted
someone
to treat
me like I was made
of them.

     *—But you are not my crown.*

All the jewels
in this world
couldn't convince
me to stop
looking for you,
but I must admit
the stars
have certainly come
close.

Imagine:

your smile
pressed
against
mine.

Funny how
I have never heard your
laugh,
and
I have never touched your
face,
but I still know
that you are the most
wondrous creation
in the
entire
universe.

I think we are born
with all of the love
we will ever possess
tucked away
in our hearts.

Some will love
themselves,
some will love
things,
some will hoard love away
so every word they
speak stings.

The risk we take
is deciding who
we give our love to.

*—Is it worth it?*

Artemis might've approved
once,
but
she learned her lesson
the hard way,
and I have,
as of yet,
not learned a thing.

You will come
one day,
bright as the morning
sun,
and then this night
will end,

all
in its own
time.

I try to imagine your arms around me,
lifting me up, out of this oblivion.
I try to imagine you kissing my
mouth, as sweet and smooth as
Kentucky bourbon, but
it's hard to do
when
all
I've
ever
known
are bitter goodbyes and
burning saltwater.

The hardest part
was breaking,
seeing that
I wasn't enough
for all those before.

The best part
was learning
that I might
maybe, possibly, hopefully
be worth
something to you.

But
what if I'm not?

How will I explain
why I was never interested
in love
before?
How
could I tell them
the truth?

CARTON

How will I explain
to them
that I thought
I was
unlovable,
so
I acted like
I was happy
with being .
alone?

      *—This is going to hurt.*

There have been some
before;
they were flashes of light,
glimpses of brilliance.

They were not the real deal.

They were lab made,
something Edison or Tesla or Westinghouse
would patent,
nowhere near
as lonesome
or as fantastic
as the stars above.

I can only hope
you are as constant.

What if I am stuck
with these
memories, these substitutes,
these imposters?
What if they are
the closest I ever get
to you?

What if our timing was off?
What if we've already
met
and kissed
and loved
and lost?

I think about her,
the me
I used to be,
the me that I left on
the floor
with the dirty laundry.

I don't think
I would know her
if I saw
her
today.

There are pieces of her
still alive
inside,
pieces of that little
girl
I used to be,
the one who folded her
hands and prayed
for a prince,
for a hero,
for a you.

She is still here,
grape-jam-smudged,
creek-water-soaked,
her daddy's little girl,
please, please, *please*

don't break her heart.

I wonder sometimes if
maybe,
maybe,
maybe you never existed
at all.

*Kintsugi.*

It means
"golden joinery."

What if we never collide?
What if we are magnets
forever circling and unable
to touch, to have, to hold?
What if this longing is the closest
I ever get?

Life without you
is a silent film,
black and white
with subtitles.

It's still beautiful,
yes,
but
not enough to
satisfy.

CARTON

Maybe I've already missed you;
maybe I looked down
for a moment too long,
just as you fell.
Maybe all I have left
are wounds
and feathers
and dreams
of what we might've been.

What if I looked away
and missed
my shooting star?

Self-love is a good thing to have;
it must come before anything else.

But I would still like
to be told
how beautiful
I am, inside and out,
not left to
whisper it
to myself
every night.

I love me;
yes,
it is a new thing,
so
*be patient*:
I am still
getting used to
the idea
that someone else
could love me
too.

I must remember that
someday,
they will lose my
picture,
and they will lose
my tears
to the air.

I must remember that
someday,
by my words
and
by my story,
I will live
forever.

You and I deserve the soft things,
the sweet things,
the warm things;
you and I deserve more than
we have accepted
this far.

Many of us
have wasted
entire lifetimes
believing that we are
too broken
to be
loved.

   —*Let the healing start here.*

I know who I am.

I know
I would survive
and
that this
won't break me.

But the ache will stay
regardless.

I don't need you,
or cupcakes,
or poetry,
or the interstate
to be complete,
but
my heart, my tongue,
my soul, my spirit,
they are
so restless
as of late.

I do not *need* you.
I *want* you.

With everything
that I am.
*I want you.*

There was a boy
who said that
I have a
heart of steel.

I
didn't
know
what
to
say
then.

Now I know that Cupid
will need his strongest
arrow; after all, I
won't fall
for just
anyone.

Where should I
start looking?

I want to feel you against me,
but my pillow
and the wind
will do
for now.

You and I
won't have
love at first sight.
I'm too afraid
for that.

It will take time,
but one day
the curtains will
open, and
you will see
me,
arms open,
waiting for you.

This feeling will grow
slowly,
as sturdy as
an oak tree,
and it will
last
a thousand times
as long.

Are you hiding in a face
I see every day
on the street?
Are you kissing someone else,
wondering if they're me?

The mountains are all around,
and the river is at my side.
The trees are perfect
paintbrush tips,
stretching
up and up to the sky.
I think you would like it
here,
where phones don't work
and gasoline is hard
to find,
where the forest
and I are one,
where I am
most alive.

I love you,
and
I might not
even know you
yet.

Long ago,
Helen's face launched
a thousand ships.

How could that be?

How could one woman
send so many
across the sea,
but I cannot find a soul
in all this world
to miss me?

There was a man
at the mall;
he looked at me and smiled,
his eyes soft.
There was quiet in his soul;
I wondered how.

Then a woman
took his hand

and I knew.

I wonder over
what I've put my body through,
what I have survived and endured
for others,
all of the pain and sorrow and regret.

You'd never ask those things of me.

I'll never do
such horrible things
to me
ever again.

Even though
you wouldn't ask
me to,
be sure that
I wouldn't,

not even for you.

*Kintsugi,*
I think that's what we will be,
the pair of us
pieces
of a broken vessel
soon to be
filled with devotion and desire,
and all of our edges
will fit together—
not perfectly, no—
but golden all the same.

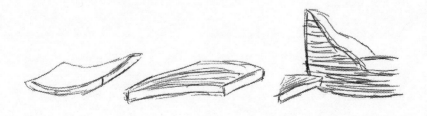

Even if I did
manage to put myself
back together,
there would still be
fragments
that I couldn't find
without your
help.

I carved my initials
down at the Clearwater,
on a tree
two hundred years old.
Just mine alone
for now.

I know that it makes no sense,
but your
hands
on my body
would make all
of this
pain,
this heartbreak,
this searching,
worth it.

There was a man
in a movie.
I liked
his eyes
(they were kind),
and his laugh
too,
but I doubt we'll ever
meet.

Someday
you will be here
to catch every tear
I cry.
You'll be here
to kiss the tears away
and remind me
that I am stronger
for
letting them
fall.

Perhaps
another time,
another place,
someplace
where there
is more time.

We must've been there
when the universe was born,
you and I,
but I don't know what you look
like
now, or
if you love me still.

The ancient Greeks
told a story
about Zeus,
how he feared humans
so much
that
he broke each one
into two halves
and condemned them to look
for each other
forever.

—*They claim this is how soul mates are made.*

Can you imagine
striking such fear
into a god
that he would
rend
an entire species
to keep us
apart?

You see,
we have been apart
for so long
because
we are too strong
together.

I am too cynical
with happiness,
too critical
with love.
I hope I haven't
passed you over
because
I was too broken
for too long.

I think we've already met,
before the earth existed,
before Orion walked
the winter sky.

He treated me like a
bouquet,
pretty and short-lived,
never to last;
but you,
no, *never*,
you will touch me
like a garden,
breathing on my roots and
feeding me,
patiently
clearing away
my dying parts
and smiling on my blooms
when I finally reach
for the
sky.

The sky isn't blue,
and neither is the sea.

These change by the day,
by the minute, by the hour;
they change come the snow
or the morning rain shower.
Sometimes they are gray
and violent, stirred up;
sometimes they are
black
as the coffee in my cup.

I've seen them green too,
as rich as a bruise;
they've been every color
since I lost my muse.

So no, I say,
neither are blue,
and that is how I found
that I could live happily
without
him around.

— to "Blue"

I watch the planes
blinking like tears
in the night sky.
I wonder if you're on one,
gazing down at the lights below,
so
I say a prayer
for each one that goes by
just in case.

No one is made
for anyone else;
we are made for ourselves,
made to be happy.
We are made
to share joy with
those we love,
and I myself
wholly wish
to share every happiness
with you.

You're already complete,
and I am too.
You cannot fix me,
and
I cannot fix you,
but
it would be easier to
put ourselves
back together
if I held the pieces
and you added the glue.

    *—We will save ourselves with each other's help.*

I *know* you won't care
how I look,
but I am still
so nervous;
others before you
have taught me
to be
this way.

I want you so much that
my breath catches,
my mouth
wants to say your name,
to twine
around those syllables
as sweet as honey;
I want to sigh them
so softly
that the candle's
flame barely flutters
against the dark
and my demons
flee
at the sound.

But all I have are books and
movies and songs
to tell me what that might
be like.

They say that love
does not boast,
but when I see you,
the birds
will fall silent
and the universe
will hold its breath
as I sing for you.
I will tell everyone
that
I have finally found
what the fairy tales
spoke of.

Also,
our love will be
quiet,
just ours,
something that only
the grass
beneath us
knows.

I will love
you
in every way that I can,
in every way that
this world
and the next world too
have ever known.

There was a girl
with golden hair
(like finished wheat)
in Tuscaloosa,
and every time that song comes on,
I wonder if she found what
we always talked about
late at night.

I haven't yet.

—*Where are you?*

There was a boy
who called me "sweet" and "pretty,"
but he took me like a shot,
like I was something to
consume quickly; he
even took a chaser
the moment
I was gone.

That's how I learned
that
plain decency
and acting grown,
that kindness and respect,
don't mean
that someone is
"the one."

Love
is not something you
earn;
it is not a prize
to be won.

—*You don't have to give yourself away.*

I am wine,
waiting to be sipped,
full and rich,
hidden, tucked away,
ever
waiting to paint your
lips.

There is a knot
in my belly,
warm and hard
to ignore;
no amount of daydreaming
will make it subside.

I am hungry
for the first time
in my life.

I want to feel you inside me,
deep, embedded;
I hunger for your touch,
but there is no face,
no voice
for me to give you.

I am at the edge,
imagining
your arms holding me,
but I don't know their
color, their strength,
and it ebbs away.
I am left too warm
and too cold,
my soul
rubbed raw.

The cherry blossoms
outside my bedroom window
are coming in,
and I feel young again,
free.
I want to comb their petals
into my hair,
want to smell them on you,
and want to compare their softness
to your skin.
I wonder what you'd do
if we rested in them
together.

I want to bite something—
a pillow, an apple,
your lips.

I am not who I was
at the beginning.

How will you recognize me?

The tiles echo as
I cry.
Outside
they don't care;
the party continues
and the whole house
shakes.

 —*What are you doing tonight?*

I drove to Chincoteague,
curious to see
the horses that live
on cord grass, salt, and poison ivy,
but they were sold
one by one,
these wild things
of the sea,
and I knew
a hundred years ago
they didn't survive the wreckage
for an ending like this.

Neither did I.

I want to go home,
but that place is yet to
be discovered.

The train sped
past.
I stood in its wind
and remembered another train
in West Virginia,
hauling coal,
and the tiny shacks there
so small and
filled with
golden warmth,
where
the hills, like arms,
embrace them.

If you are my mountains,
then I will be your
home
too.

I will memorize
every freckle,
every scar.
I will burn with you
the way stars do,
and you will
be my home.

CARTON

Be welcome and arrive
with muddy
shoes and
stories to tell.
I hope you track into
~~this heart~~ this house
of mine
and make yourself at
home.

Outside my window
there is a wind chime
from far away
where I visited.

I watch it spin,
and I pretend
that it does not sing
for Ohio's wind.
Instead I pretend
the breeze that combs
through it
came from elsewhere;
maybe it brushed against
you,
where the rest of my life
I'll one day spend.

I am like
a lamp,
ornate and antique,
dusty and traveled,
with chips and cracks.
I might be dull now,
but I would shine
so brightly
if you would light
me up.

On the bus
in Columbus,
I imagine us sitting
side by side,
the buildings blocking out
the sun,
and
I think about the man
beside me.

I wonder,
*If I touch his pinky finger*
*with mine,*
*will he pull*
*away?*

I didn't try.

The sunset
would be more beautiful
if I were seeing it
reflected in your
eyes.

I mourned those horses on Virginia's coast, the ones born captive who escaped to run free; I thought of their roundup, of their breaking and told Grandmother my fear. And she nodded slowly, eyes green like mine: "I don't think that any-thing, once wild, can ever be tame again."

Where are you?
Is this all there is?
The hoping
for a hand to hold,
a place to hide,
lips to taste,
someone to lie beside?

Our atoms were close
to each other
at the beginning of time.

—*That's where we began.*

Like ever-flowing water
that fills the falls,
in tumultuous chaos and thunder
or the evening wind soft
that carries cricket calls
and caresses the gilded fields,
so passionate, so gentle
is my love for you.

—So passionate, so gentle.

There was a man.
He flagged me down outside
Billings.
He had the grayest eyes
I'd ever seen
and leathered skin,
far older than mine.
He invited me to stay awhile,
and he shared
his own searching stories.

He was kind.
He was alone.
He was me.

I kept driving.

Every person
I have ever met
has a story
to which I will
never be privy.

I think about that
when I drive at night,
when I pass through
little towns
dark but for streetlights.
I think about that
in the hotel room
when I hear the door
across the hall close,
and the silence resumes.

I think about
all the stoops
I'll never cross,
of all the air I'll never
taste,
and the people
whose voices
I'll never hear.

I think about
what a miracle it would be
to find you
in all of this glorious
chaos.

The tires are hot,
*gravel, pavement, dirt, repeat,*
but I know you're out there
waiting
for someone,
someone
who is me.

You will recognize me
far from these
lights and
these streets;
you will recognize me
and know
that our souls were
long ago
split from the
same comet.

Our skin
touching,
our bodies a current,
we are endless,
as timeless as the river yonder,
and our love will be
just as deep.

I think of those mountains,
the ones in Idaho,
where my cousins
fish the river.

I am alive there,
sure.
But that isolation,
that tumbling, breathing,
wild land,
oh,
how it is in my veins,
oh,
the way that you
are in my heart.

My life has been a desert
this whole time—
hot and golden and marvelous—
but I am thirsty now
and just realized

I've never tasted water before.

Sometimes when I drive,
I have to turn off
the radio
because every song
is about you, about
us,
but none of those songs
have come true
yet.

I want to breathe
you in
again
and again
and again.

Love cannot be bargained for, no;
love is patient and kind,
never abused
and
never twisted.

To love simply for love's
sake
and for no other reason
is why we exist.

CARTON

There was a girl,
a ballerina I knew,
and as I watched,
she took
off her shoes, and
I stared and stared at the blood and the cracks, at the broken skin
stained with greens
and blacks.
She caught my eye; she cleared her throat.
"To love something is not beautiful, you
see, but what
you get out
of it is
the most
beautiful
thing
of all."

We are not born
to accomplish
love;
we are not born
to earn it.
It is not a prize.

We are born
to have love,
simply,
and to give it away
freely
for all of our
lives.

I want to tell you
everything,
but
but
but
bu

The curtains are heavy
over the stage as
they tune up;
a faint pizzicato
reaches the
balcony.

I've come too far,
too far for you
to follow me back,
but I know that I would stay
if I found you here.

      —*This is why Mozart wrote music.*

I wonder if you are
a celebrity
with
loyal fans,
someone with a schedule
to keep,
someone who runs
on too little sleep,
but when you do
at last lie down,
you see *you*
standing with *me*,
and you think
about what maybe
we
might could be.

But then
the lights come on,
and you forget
about me
and what we
might could be
all over
again.

It is midmorning at the coffee
house, and
I think it's time for a trip.

CARTON

Now I see
the truth:
love isn't a burden;
no,
it is the keeper
of youth.

I will follow you anywhere,
anywhere, anywhere.

I don't want a
stand-in
or
a good time.
I want
to stand with you
for all time.

There was a man
by the lake in Saugatuck,
and my breath caught
with
embarrassment,
nervousness.

I looked away and back,
but he was gone.

Maybe
I missed you again.

I walked out among the waves
to the lighthouse
as the evening fell.
I saw boys
jumping from the peer,
showing off like
young buck deer,
and the girls
giggled and laughed
like sea nymphs
escaped from ship prows,
painted purple and gold in the
fading sun.

I turned away,
my throat tight
and towel tighter.

You will arrive,
and the sky will turn yellow,
the way it does before
a storm.
And the air will fall
heavy in my chest,
weighted with
meaning.

The sirens will wail,
and thunder
will grind at my ribs.

But
my greatest fear
is that

you won't feel
a thing.

I dreamed last night
of a ball and
a dress,
and you were there.
We escaped
to the balcony,
out into the garden;
gooseflesh rose on
my skin
when you took my hand
and we ran into
the hedges, toward the mountains,
past the lake,
and into the sky.
Everything fell away,
and the stars had
a castle ready for us
there.

Looking for
you is like wading,
going by touch,
not by sight,
floating
and treading
and gasping; I
panic a little as my feet
can't touch this far out.

TO YOU *in the* NIGHT

Maybe you are an angel,
and that's why
I feel you so
closely;
maybe God's hand slipped,
maybe you were sent
to watch over me.

Maybe
we may
never touch.

There is a song
about two lovers breathing,
and
sometimes,
when I am in Astoria,
driving across that bridge
so high up,
I taste you
through the open car windows
where the river meets the sea,
and my eyes fill.

—*There is no peace for me on the road anymore.*

The
Pacific
giggled,
and my
soul,

it
smiled
back,
quite
shy

and
unsure
of how
to act.
She roiled at my feet,
and a voice older than religion,
older than all of this world's
sorrows
and joys, tickled my toes
and hugged my soul close:

*It will be worth it.*

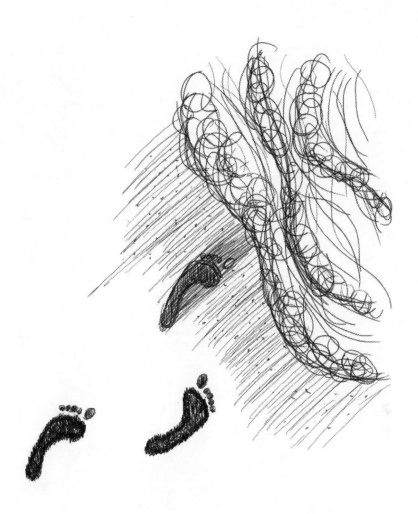

I used to think
there was nothing
but the road,
nothing but the adventure,
the freedom.
*Part of that is still true,*
but now I know
it's okay
to feel this way
too.

 —*My life isn't for everyone.*

I want to kiss
that area beneath your
ear,
long and soft and gentle,
across your jaw
and up your temple.
I want to touch you
the way people touch
fragile things.

You are not
what has happened,
no.
You are not ephemeral
that way,
no.
You are everlasting
and precious and worthy
of every happiness
the world could provide
and more.

I will do all I can
to keep your cup
full.

Every time you fall,
you will rise again,
like the forest
after the fire,
like the sun
after the night,
and
I will help you
up,
I will dust you off,
I will clean your wounds
if you will do
the same
for me.

We will
have that love,
the kind
they will sing
about
a thousand years
from now.

In a world
where I have been forced
to be tough,
you are my
weakness,
and that means
someday
you will be
my greatest
strength
too.

The whole world
is cheering us on;
the whole world
is keeping us apart.

Isn't it wild
that our fingers entwine
just right,
and our faces tuck against
each other's necks,
out of sight.
Or maybe it's how
our chins rest on shoulders
and our hands
can so gently
wipe away tears,
and just a few
words
can
quiet
our deepest fears?

Isn't it wild
how humans
are perfectly shaped
to be held?

They say that
you will find love
when you aren't
looking for it,
so
I will close my eyes
for a little
while
and wait
for you
to wake me up.

When the snow falls silent,
and
not a wind stirs
the night,
I pause under
the streetlamps
and take in the sight.
I imagine
you smiling,
you laughing,
breath foggy and light,
and I wonder if one day
we, together,
might enjoy
such a night.

I learned a new word
today
as I studied
my ancestry:

*Mo shíorghrá.*

It's time for a trip.

What does firelight
look like on
your skin?
What does Guinness
taste like
on
your
tongue?

I want to speak
like Ophelia.
I want to
leave flowers,
fresh and new,
in our bed.
My love,
I want to share
the finest of
my daisies
with you.

We should walk through
the cold sea haar.
I hope you know
I have come this far,
and I'll go farther still
until
I find you.

I am floating
in the lake,
weightless,
between the water
and the sky.
I imagine that
if I sit up,
you will be waiting for me
on the shore,
or maybe
you will be swimming
out to
join
me.

They don't understand my
madness;
they can't see what
I know.
All I can tell them
is someday I'll stop,
but
until then,
I must go.

I have obsessed
over
how you might do
something
as simple as use
a mug.

Is it between your hands
to warm them,
or is it held
by the handle?
Are you the coffee
type?
Black or with cream?
Or perhaps it's
tea? If so,
is it black, or
is it green?
Or
maybe you prefer
milk
or orange
juice.

What color is it,
your favorite mug?

      *—I want to know every little thing.*

There was an old woman.
She told me that
her neighbor was
playing pass with
a friend
when the ball bounced
over the fence.

It hit her leg.

She said that
from that moment
on, she knew he was
"the one."

*If only it all
were so simple,*
I thought.

She smiled.
"Love *is* simple,
but only
if you allow it
to be."

Let the rain
slick our bodies
while I kiss you
and
bury
my face
in your neck.

I want to hold
you every night.
I want to
kiss you
in the
morning's light.

*Mo shíorghrá.*

It means
"my eternal love" or "soul mate."

Oh,
I want to see you
under Liverpool's lamps
swathed in fog,
hair damp
and unkempt.
I want to see you
smiling back at me
in a marketplace,
a bit of spice
smeared
across your face.
Yes,
I want to see you
well-rested,
eyes bright,
between white linen sheets
and the smell of brine
kissing your skin
with me.

Oh,
I want to see you.

Sometimes
I try to count
the breaths
that I might take
before I meet you.

Is it a million;
is it 10,000?

Is it one?

I'm certain you're out there
kissing someone,
hoping that they are me,
and when I find you,
I'll show you all the
things you've missed.

I know in my bones,
you'll show me too.

## Epilogue

If I ever find the one,
the one who eclipses the setting sun,
the one who makes all else fade away,
the one I'll wake up to every day,
then I will claim this book,
this first love letter.
I'll claim it for worse,
or I'll claim it for better.
You see, I don't want to be loved
for where I've been or how I look.
I want to be loved for who I am,
and furthermore, not
for writing this book.
So until that day comes,
I will travel and write
such love letters to you,
to you in the night.